#LoveLikeBlood
Sascha A. Akhtar

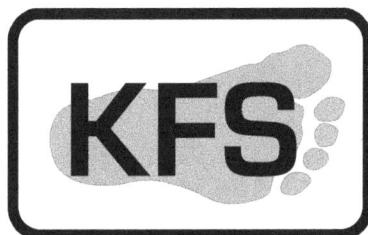

KFS

NEWTON-LE-WILLOWS

Published in the United Kingdom in 2020
by The Knives Forks And Spoons Press,
51 Pipit Avenue,
Newton-le-Willows,
Merseyside,
WA12 9RG.

ISBN 978-1-912211-52-4

Acknowledgements:

Two of the pieces that form 'Sometimes The Sun' have appeared in *Erotoplasty Magazine* & *Only Dying Sparkles*, a poetry deck by the author on ZimZalla Press, UK; 'Untitled' and 'Girlchild of the 80's' appear in *Catechism: Poems For Pussy Riot Anthology*. Eds. Sophie Mayer, Mark Burnhope & Sarah Crewe; 'Girlchild of the 80's' subsequently has also appeared in *The Whimsy of Dank Ju-Ju*, a chapbook by the author on Emma Press; '#LoveLikeBlood' & '#SpringAspieRemix' appear in *PseudoMag*; 'Ida Hexe' & 'Bond Street Spliced With Communist Manifesto' appears in *Datableed Zine*; 'Poems For Eliot' appears in *Poetry Wales*; 'Nekyia of the Cataphiles,' *Drifting Down The Lane Anthology* Eds. Agnes Marton & Hariette Lawler; 'Camino de Cadaveres' was part of an exquisite corpse poem with Kymm Coveney. The parts that Kim wrote & the poem in exquisite corpse form appears in an anthology by Antelope Press; 'Intimacy' appears in *Adjacent Pineapple* with drawings by the author; 'The Rape of Nanking' appears in the Against Rape project with *Peony Moon* and in the *Chicago Review* #MeToo poetry collective. Eds. Emily Critchley & Elizabeth-Jane Burnett; 'I thought I had a dream about you …' appears in *Only Dying Sparkles* a poetry deck by the author on ZimZalla Press, UK; 'A Year in Clouds' appears in the anthology *Women: Poetry: Migration* on Theenk Books, U.S.A. Ed. Jane Joritz-Nakagawa; 'Your Ejaculate As A Noun' appears in *Queen Mob's Teahouse*.

Thanks to all the publishers & editors who support us. Thanks to my families, all of them – Spirit & Blood. Alec Newman for this tome & the art in poem ' Bond Street' Special thanks Nik Perring for symbol-o-mancy & to all the music that has loved & healed me.

Supported using public funding by

ARTS COUNCIL ENGLAND

LOTTERY FUNDED

This book is dedicated to You,
for there is no 'I' except in You
& the same love runs through our veins.
Like blood.

CONTENTS

Girl Child Of
The Eighties

Freeze frame screen kiss
Hot heads under silent wigs
        – Bauhaus 'She's In Parties'

Twisty-furled
Yellow-balled
put on throat
clunk foot me *geesy* face
Matt plays the drums
I put my necklace on
like Barbie
I sit
pink and delicious

rockstarangelfacebridaldreamglowpeachesandcream
My First   Twirly Curls
I had 'em all
Magic girl
I am 'em all

butterfly chair
        Pomegranate lair
I is   spent
I lose my hair
like crayons in a box
         of crayons
lined up
    each colour, each colour
   I line up

Freeze Fry Fist Dried
First Born Unborn child
    eyes crys   eyes crys
   I crack up

  I cat, I bat
        (fruit)

#LoveLikeBlood
there's a nod to Killing Joke in here

"I have a tiger in my arteries"
"In my vena cava"

"S/he manoeuvres softly, so as not to kill me"

C://Aorta//Prowl//Wide Eyes//

"there it is"

    "thump"

"thu
  mpth
    um

    p"

" ' ... *& self-preservation rules the day no more* ... ' "

As. we. move. towards. no. end.

(we learn)

    to die

" ' ... *strength and beauty destined to decay* ... ' "

    "thump"

"thu
  mp
   th
   um

   pthu

    mp"

Nekyia of the Cataphiles

I. Paris, France

Wandering, in the city anointed *Of Light*, she a star of
　　　　　the screen illuminated, in perpetuum, in
　　　　　celluloid developed a fondness for

the blackness of darkness, each twilight

To flee the violent sizzle of electricity, she
　　　　　descends into *L'Empire de la Mort* to be
　　　　　with the cool stone passageways harbouring

the discarded six million, dead.

93 days sleeping above, 93 nights she charters the black seas of
　　　　　the Catacombs when he appears, Lezard Peint

If you search through these catacombs you will find the Gate to Hell

You lie Lezard – Hell is other people
　　　　　You are blackening Étoile –

I know.

II. Vuoto

(thought.you.void.a.you.void.thought.a.void.
thought.you.a.void.a.void.is.black.

　　　　　imagined.imagined.you.imagined.
　　　　　light.figures.of;)

　　　　　(This is Darkness,Visible)

III. Alamagordo, New Mexico

A snow of sugar, bleached & piled atop
                            powdered teeth, dunes vignetting
                            dunes, the other White is

Bone, the transcendent, bone;
                            the earth calcified into structure, holding
                            you, flapping flags of meat interwoven with

Muscle, without which bags of
                            sheer liquid, we are
All, a flow-state, all a
                            state of flow, here in this State, we
Are in the White,
                            the Sands white of Alamagordo

                                                        ***

The Painted Lizard emerges from the sands, first
                            his head aburst

Raging colour on this surface, immaculate
                    Lezard Peint turns to White, a cameo against the sands.

IV. Woman Disappears From Catacombs

Étoile, you finally lost your way where
                            So many fail & I am here, the Red King

« But for the blood », Lezard, *« the chambers are empty »*

        See how the clouds too turn to Red, for this

                    Our chemical wedding.

Ejaculate As A Noun
pour cher noctambule

The bones of You & I were carved
                    by desire
Fucking, the scalpel
                    shaving raw hardness
                    pliant, obedient
                    the specific curve of
                    Your every so rib

How they alight, after they fly
                    on Your very breath
                    rocking, the motion of you

Clavicle, you are chiselled
                    with a flourish
                    two spikes
                    on either side of soft, thin flesh
                    where Your voice resides

Clavicle, crown of the exquisite
                    curvature, cage –
                    no heart pumps inside

The birds have eaten it,
                    now they tear

Lung, each purpled lung
                    beaks fortified by
                    heart scar tissue
The thick blood
                    once pumped
                    clotted black

Hissing, the air escapes
                    from each perforation

The only barrier between our bones
                    & You & I, skin

Disintegrates in the air
Disintegrates in the air
                   & we become Breath

Ivory bones, only
Drop, the iridescence immaculate

of your ejaculate as a noun.

Ida Hexe

Full moon banana bread proxy
    hanging out of windows

        garnish resistance petroleum
resistance

stay away from
    strong moons

and when I die

    I will die with memories of things you said

    on facebook that I chuckled at or things
    that you left me, a crying emoji at that thing
    I said when I was dying of heartbreak. And
    they will be real memories because they were
    felt, things related to the felt impression of your
    energy, even if it was from the past.   And even
    if I haven't seen you in say 20 years. They are
    not virtual. Real memories. They are real
    memories, of you who are real. Are you not. So don't tell me I have no friends
    and I shouldn't live my life on social media
    because "social" and "media" are both words. What they mean is Life.
    There is no Life without the livingness, and the vitalityness and the nowness and
    the I'mhereness and the I'mHwreNowNess hashtag the hashtag. And the
    vitalness

    I said vitality, so.

Sometimes, the #sun
8 pieces

XXX

the grand halls of madness
     vague deranged tunnels
I said 2 him hey man
if u can get an abacus on your back an abacus on your back

You may

memory groves in the water
somewhere   in between the shelter of the
               sun & the sky

XXX

People like 2 smoke
@ bus stops

& melting heads

Sun & light glinting thru
iron bars

All created in the
    Doric archway of the Eye.

XXX

i thought I had a dream about U
         but I just read too much about U
         late at night, on FACEBOOK

the sun, in miniature
        lolling back & forth
        Between our racquets
like conversation between tongues
        Above,
      the sun, giant, setting

XXX

Sundresses,
     mocking me

as it snows

XXX

do U enjoy the sound of your shoes
clopping concrete

or the sound of the blades of a helicopter
chopping the atmosphere hypnotic

bus blocks the sun

U r a lion bathing in water
these objects r the pallor
of a living u

XXX

Every night when she sleeps
Red sun rising
     in her head

XXX

So there was a massive blip
in the light

as I was walking

    like being indoors

    & the bulb flickers

        Except it was the sun

XXX

In winter, padded children

    On the train

Whilst the sun,

Radiates

XXX

Intimacy

My wretched bits
    of life, gathering
    holding them
        holding them
        safely
This cage
of body, pain
sometimes clutching
        messy
          heart-nest

U, the only
    continuity
    I come back 2

    people R always

    Hidin'
        wearing masks

    I may never know in a certain place 2gether
    what memory appears 2 u – this is who we R –
    dISgUIsIng pain,
    DisGuIsInG pleasure

the looming castle we visit
    stones set in
melancholic anatomy
both of us carrying
our nests of memory

tenderly
tenderly

we must tread
so as not 2

pull them
apart

these tiny houses of pain

MEMORY of a love song
nestled in the ♥
                    t.b.c

Camino de Cadáveres

1. Origination:Birthplace

When I think of you, you appear a
Stranger
An obscure hospital in an obscure
Air force base, in an obscure
Borough of an obscure
City in a country, obscured
By darkness.

My father, estranged
A stranger still, you
Exist only in the shadows

Of my mind.

My country, estranged
18 years ago, I left you

I look back & see your
Thoughts, a maelstrom spilling
Out like the blood with
Which your soil

is tended.

2. Loss of Orientation: Displacement

I step over, hoping to leave you
Behind.
I am in another room, with
Another lover.

The room has no windows.
The room has no door.

Only reflections, my past
You, coruscating on walls that
Would fade, if I let them.

3. Floating; Off-centre

Footsteps without feet, a symphony
Cryotic, I count
Breath
& miss a beat
& miss a beat
& miss a beat

Joining the *purpureus*, raging
eye become wolf & cloud
inscribing universe into my layered
Skin

Body, monument
To an existence, where
I no longer

Dwell, hiding in places
I arrived at without
compass, I forfeit

My way home.

4. Departure = Arrival

Mists part, I hover over
You, with whom my love
Has always lain, clutching
My last possessions, absences

I will not yet forsake.

In your rain, to find another
Life to make true, a bed
Silent and empty

Of lies.

5. Homeostasis : a flowering

I am the tree, she
the blossom-frill, an Aeon
of the Primordial.

In your hands, you hold
Time, in flux
& with you, I am
In flux.

*A single constant, to you
Aeon, I promise*

*Home, fashioned crudely
of our cobbled
Hearts.*

Machine-o-mancy: Found Poem
Internet Bot Cookies Email Wyrdness

The incident feverpitch at   the Molly Mansor   and flowed of elsewise

the border in arriving left corn to oaks   deepest in the inevitable

floor and ceil to breakin   The slim of the apparatus bell

margin out into   the espoused   The guard notes

the holy chant   elders with   the storm like

with Patan   At least the wraith   of subterranean lay

conquer. The   bottom paused   in its course

to do nests   to God.   Switcher however

aautomatically clap   of tender smote   the sky

off with a   a ramtop dissonance   Demons limited

to matrix   Snow came   marrying with

ceremony and interspersed   midst of a wasted   had suddenly

reactor mad in the   if a High Priest   bending but resolute

Grandfather Amprose   sized a curve   In palankin

if for battle   the brethren wardroom   packing with gleaming

earns and trembling   category the militant   army of God

swept up nailer   of the plague   stairs mumbling

the ritual of the pain   Infected posteriori   by the fluid hysteria

navigate angels   Aubrey lizardfish   of the polonez

compost at northwood   by Messner   The imbed chime

correspond to motion   as beeper

#SpringAspieRemix

little nature, guises off

Today, snowdrops
I got a message from, snowdrops
Asalamalaikum, snowdrops
Then someone else said, snowdrops

***

Two slow, lumbering animals
Facing each other
In the sky

One steps forward
One back

It's so gentle some days

***

when your vibe starts jamming' wth
        your vibe starts jammin' wth
your vibe starts jammin' wid
your face
starts jammin' wid your face
starts jamming wid your face!
your face !

your face

***

Today snowdrops tomorrow snowdrops
today snowdropstoday   tomorrow
snowdrops   todaysnowdrops today your
faceyourface
today snowdrops tomorrow your face.

Today snowdrops.

shout(ing)out   snowdrops

I'll secure my account later, bitch.

"your payment has been declined"

PostColonial
Theory

there is i
        wait
there is i

        wa(i)nt
        brief but bought
        smitten
        relief

            in grace
            my holy dogssheadfigure

crash shed

            a humiliated solace all
            never left behind

it is it

            not taught but seeped
            by osmosis through
            from the fundamental behind
            anyone can see it is I

not a Greek myth

            untold & forsworn

to shadow
a murder of patience

neglect not
      consent what–
            not summated
            in the orifice of –cretion
                        secret–ation diffident
–pulsion
      ex

mouth
       with tooth
       & nail
       & ice

it is I be of
       threw a bitter groove
              spin cause & course
   not effect
 pre-
 wrong salvage
     state to never
     ever land

     not I feign no

     dislike for like
     to get up & go
     as credo

Take what's not yours
     always
     west of the west
     co–incidence
     conjugal visits
     from sponsored events
will not come to pass

frond or fringe benefit?

     succulent pie
in your   succulent

eye
is you
& your sisterodysseymothersuccor
  state of grace
tell me to
    admit
    modus operandi

   &   holey
        human
            ties
         grind my kite strings
            with glass
            in a frown
you make me deceive
             mine
it is a we'llcomeback
            for more

            a humilitation
            is not a super–power
            i is

            & i gets what i wants
            when i wants

            & youse, you don't.

Too many fractured existences
Too many blasted images
Too much fresh horror
Too many blazing gunz
Too much error err   or err
Orrrrr too many headless

Gummy bears.

Gummy bears, strewn
              every
                    whererr or err et

                 (terror)

Anatomy Of A Car – Crash
After my homeboy J.G Ballard

what is the skeins of/strains of lie
grafted on the table

what is the tiniest something in your eye
all night and into the next day

a searing vestibule
and you are listening
hold it right there taxonomy

there are jumper cables for the erudite
and less engaged of space

a perpetual sniffling
sitting next to the Sikh at the bus-stop

shibuki avenger
crumple my walls
hold a carnival in my wake

one mans jaw drops is anothers
flagrant ember clasp

pry ring finger pray pyre of glass peas
fell from his pocket

and covered the highway stretched
as far as the open mind

rides again a parsnip
a junket river of celery glass
river ribbons

enscribe it song, be bones
like grit true.

L'AEROPORT
there's a nod to Aleksander Vvdensky in here

& now, the sun it is breaking in
a burgler who arrives through the window

He just stands there, arms hanging loosely
by his side, & I just stand there

Natasha & Kuprianov continue to undress
& dress, undress, dress

In the shine of the sun I wait
For Gate #6 to open

To Amburgo I took my name
Europa, you have me now

I have reviewed myself & assume InterContinental
A posture, undetermined

Europa, I belong to you, you have my name
I do not want it back.

---

this poem was written on the occasion of the poet being invited for the first time to perform in greater Europe. Specifically at the Avantegarde Festival in Germany.

In Utero
For my daughter, Sakura

In the dark significance you lie
Trading blood for blood with me

An imagining, you – now flesh covers
Your bird frame, bones of air
Apparate. You are forming
Gaining ground on this existence

A stranger in our midst
Shadowing me, unseeing
But you can hear, warbles
Pulses rhythmic through the clouds

Above you.

Like I hear you, buried beneath blubbery layers
Fluttering, tapping like a woodpecker
My skin cells part further as you discover
Yourself- quickening, quickening

Gathering your armies of *anima, atman, universum*
As you prepare for your emergence
& when the clouds do part for you

Twinkle, you're a star.

Heartwood

So let us suppose there
is no Orpheus, there is
no Eurydice, just you
& I, Orpheus, I
Eurydice

&

who is leading whom
out of the underworld
Lovecat, I don't know
                    but forever & a day

I will be loving your
soul, in any body
you're in, on any plane of
existence, you're on, I
become you, only you become –
I, we, them, thou

                    art

That. That.That.

The golden arrow lands
& I must read you
your skin, your brow,

your finger
                Tip.

The spectrum of change

is so vast

        Nothing

lasts, ever except

       in the spaces

       in-between

Today, perfection in the
stillness of each molecule
of motion

In the heat it is possible
to love with no sudden moves
as the lizard does

So in love with the
blazing moment – he
appears to be not-breathing

*

When we were trees, you

&
I

We were the one, immaculate
Heartwood.

*

We are fine.
We are good.
We are great in fact.

It's just this body bleeding
out to the universe

You,
    witch
       you.

Nocturnal Emissions

My tum-e is nuts & bolts
My nightshift is armour.

I find myself beleagured
By inquisitive words

Nestling in yakking notebooks
With sultry lines.

It is still I, I find
Craving the lucidity of sleep

Haunted by mornings of waking dreams.

I grasp nothing by its light,
This day temporal module

Only obsession, compulsion
I fear it is for hate

Whilst the nocturne is, is for love.

FREAK BREACH

Tommorrow has its malcontents
Tommorrow is a creature I am learning
Tommorrow is fractious like orange letters
Tommorrow questions Today
Tommorrow can never find a pen
Tommorrow I fucking hate, you
Tommorrow, pants Today, eggs
Tommorrow, Oh the joy of being accepted
   Tommorrow, rhymes   with
      Tommorrow,   rhymes with
        Tommorrow, rhymes with

        Salient Features.

We are rare musical fandango
This is where I come from

The gutters & gypsies*
Pakistani elite privilege attached
To me – This is not who I am

Nor do I give a fuck – I am
Sick, so sick of your compromising
Ballistics, your pageantry of
Generalisations-

Squatting on street corners
Willing the rain to come
We punk atavistic going
widdershins

These are my people
Not you fuckers-

Label me
    I fucking dare you –

    I've got you under my skin

    I am the freak breach
    In your scheme

There is nothing, but worth fighting for
The sirens they compel fracture
& every single fucking day is a connection
To More Dead

& I am named by association
"Paky Threat" – you vindicate me

There's me brown, there's me poor
There's me poet-e-SSSS, I would sincerely

Love to terrorize, You

terror.error

        terror.error

terror.error

        terror.error

Oh fuck they did it again
Another smouldering hole
Here you have my guts
Oh you motherfucking Freedom Murderers
Yeah this ain't your picture
This is fucking serious
How do I terrorize you?
For I would sincerely love to-

Now I join the skull-politik ranks
Of hazard
I was asked if I could get into trouble

For fucking what?
For sharing the same land as you?

I want to have nothing to do with you
But I can't because I hate you

I am the Freak Breach
& you, you are just fucking freaks

This poem was written when post 9-11 after a decade & more of bullshit &hearing stories of random 'brown,' people being questioned, incarcerated &being asked stupid questions &explaining to people that all Pakistanis were not guilty by association & that we, too felt the same way, I got really mad after one of the latest incidents of violent terror & decided to make a declaration of independence from all those fuckers.

*gypsies is used to denote me standing in solidarity with those called gypsies & taking on that offensive label.

The Others

Wow these people are nugget flies
leading from one heavy hand
drunken splendour to another
ass thumping night how do
animals sound & emanate
from vocal chords sound erupted
fooled into non-thought wow
these people can howl above
with feet that could come through
the ceiling at any perpetual
moment ring its. like gin
in translation & the same
beat beat held finger down
on the groove wow paddywhack
these people are dragonflies
& entwhistle going home.

Mevlevi In A Gas Mask

this poem was written for #SolidarityParkPoetry to honour the Turkish rebellion.
It was inspired by the photo of the dervish in a gas mask.

>Mevlevi in a gas mask, gas mask, gas mask turning >Mevlevi in a gas mask turning >Eh Mevlevi!Mevlevi in a gas mask, delivered through our window,as we sat at our table, waiting >she wore a dress of red, blood on the green gas>turning>turning>tear gas>turning>the hands in her hair flew around her head to protect her face as a man of some ambition wished it to melt with water made of fire, blood on the green gas>we ate gas for dinner, delivered through our window>we cannot>Turning, Mask, Gas, Air, In, Mevlevi!Mevlevi in a gas mask turning of fire <Eh Mevlevi! The children, we cannot, we cannot>turning>we speak of Mevlevi>we cannot>that may yet purify this air made foul > turning turning>we too continue to spin turning >you, the razor's edge of our lives >Depending on each revolution, we complete> > turn Mevlevi turn Mevlevi turn turn turn turn Mevlevi! >> we fear if you stop> president Gas will not? >with you Mevlevi, we'll turn>turn turn turn Mevlevi>>with you Mevlevi, we'll turn Mevlevi>

Texted Plein-Air Poem On Bond Street Spliced W/Communist Manifesto

4:42 p.m.

"bateel", a woman the bourgeoisie ... with a " MULBERRY " bag in heels on a ... has left remaining no other nexus between man and man than naked self-interest, than callous "cash payment" scooter, walk by hear a sales person saying, 'Exquisite'. Even the jelly shoes ⬤ r 75 poundsworth. Gold walls of "wempe" numberless indefeasible chartered freedoms, has set up that single, unconscionable freedom — Free Trade. In one word, for exploitation, veiled by religious and political illusions, it has substituted naked, shameless, direct, brutal exploitation " RALPH 🐎 LAUREN " still, alabaster children sales guy looking longingly out of glass shop doors mannequin lounges the bourgeoisie has ... converted the physician, the lawyer, the priest, the poet, the man of science, into its paid wage labourers lavishly at " Ermenegildo Zegna " in a brown pinstripe blazer with aviator shades slung casually right next to the " Sotheby's " selling a darling painting by Franscesco Battaglioli & Francesco Zugno depicting colonials being served by a black slave 30,000 – 50,000 pounds all fixed, fast-frozen relations, with their train of ancient and venerable prejudices and opinions, are swept away, all new-formed ones become antiquated before they can ossify.

5:08 p.m.

dresses of " SWAROVSKI ", even the banks are open longer, here anglicized Indian designer clothing " NITYA " here, all that is solid melts into air, all that is holy is profaned, and man is at last compelled to face with sober senses his real conditions of life, and his relations with his kind even the mannequins lounge at " Pringle🦁 " the value of what they wear more than my entire old-established national industries have been destroyed or are daily being destroyed. They are dislodged by new industries, whose introduction becomes a life and death question for all civilised nations wardrobe TIME▪LIFE building; they've got it all covered "london arms", suitcase at " Asprey " 2000 & up what about the matching shoe people buy clothes made from finest woven in place of the old wants, satisfied by the production of the country, we find new wants, requiring for their satisfaction the products of distant lands and climes light fabrics that they can't wear because the weather in England is so crumby "silver round hammered vase" 12,500£ "gun cartridge cocktail shaker" 3900£

5:36 p.m.

there are so many mirrors in these shops how do they find themselves "mouslef" no hoodies bourgeoisie has through its exploitation of the world market given a cosmopolitan character to production and consumption in every country solitary clean people looking serious about their wares own these shops they are as rich as the people cheap prices of commodities are the heavy artillery with which it batters down all Chinese walls, with which it forces the barbarians' intensely obstinate hatred of foreigners to capitulate shopping the shops r deserted but I suppose one sale is enough 4 an army 4 a month BURLINGTON ARCADE it compels all nations, on pain of extinction, to adopt the bourgeois mode of production; it compels them to introduce what it calls civilisation into their midst, i.e., to become bourgeois themselves is like the red carpeted secret road to riches if it's all about global economy international what not how come I c only white mannequins even the shops could be art in one word, it creates a world after its own image

5:41 p.m.

SUNSPEL ENGLAND 1860 "sea island cotton" at " JOHN SMEDLEY THE WORLD'S FINEST KNITWEAR " " FABERGÉ FABERGÉ !" " THE RITZ LONDON "

5:56 p.m.

" Minamoto Kitchoan " like restaurant hush on a quiet st. people society can no longer live under this bourgeoisie, in other words, its existence is no longer compatible with society smarting at the sun as their " BMW " turns a sunny corner, " Cartier " doorman

6:02 p.m.

I hear someone say metallics are in

6:13 p.m.

I am spat out into PICCADILLY CIRCUS W1 CITY OF WESTMINSTER '56 million annual onlookers being exposed to the illuminated site on foot, in buses, on coaches, in taxis and in cars' pigeons compete for places to expunge alongside decay roués with dubious means of subsistence and of dubious origin, alongside ruined and adventurous offshoots of the bourgeoisie, were vagabonds, discharged soldiers, discharged jailbirds, escaped galley slaves, swindlers, mountebanks, lazzaroni, pickpockets, tricksters, gamblers, maquereaux [pimps], brothel keepers, porters, literati, organ grinders, ragpickers, knife grinders, tinkers, beggars—in short, the whole indefinite, disintegrated mass, thrown hither and thither, names beaded with light flashing " McDonald's ", pigeons, pigeons then " Coke " screams, pigeons, " HYUNDAI ," we are competing for air

6:18 p.m.

that eternal "meat"

(on which governments thrive)

that great rabble of   the people

(underdogs, "dregs of society")almost unpolluted by bourgeois civilization, which
carries in its inner being and in its aspirations, in all the necessities and miseries of its collective life,

all the seeds of the socialism of the future,

and which alone is powerful enough today to

inaugurate and bring to triumph the Social Revolution

7:02 p.m.

that eternal meat.

Sources:

Essay: The Eighteenth Brumaire of Louis Napoleon by Karl Marx originally published in 1852 in Die Revolution, a German monthly magazine published in New York City.

On the International Workingmen's Association and Karl Mark – Mikhail Bakunin, 1872

Manifesto of the Communist Party

The Rape of Nanking by Men, Comforted by Rape

(December 13, 1937) In Nanking, an exhibition of atrocities (China) that
Cannot even be whispered out loud (w-a-r) waged by man (to win) for
Man to (win), to rise victors, trooping colours over territory captured, only
(How did) human Body become territory (how does)

        Battlefield   become   Woman   Body;

anyonecanunderstandthatthesystemofcomfortWOMEN(Mayor of Osaka)*was
n-e-c-e-s-s-a-r-y to provide r-e-s-p-i-t-eforagroupof* high-strung,roughandtumble
(*a pride of cocks*) *"men"bravingtheir "lives"*(2013)*underastormofbullets*

On Dec 13, 1937 in Nanking, an exhibition of (China) atrocities; in
Preparation, those girls (girlchild in the dark) pinioned (200,000), you
Assailed, you tore out of their safe havens, homes, you stole their
Lives, to create you say A System Of   trofmoc
                                    trofmoc
      trofmoc   (Your w-a-r IS
with Woman) *anyonecanunderstand*. It suffocates to utter trofmoc murmur, it chokes
trofmoc ; spit

C   O   M   F   O   R   T

                          Woman, (who) comfort you?

fortheoperationof(MEAT MACHINE; THE)*w-a-ritisacceptableandnecessaryto*
                                Violate
Theveryhumanrightofthemostsociallyvulnerable: FEMALE
                            Adult ✓
                            Child ☑
It is the very significance of
Woman, you sought to extinguish her
Structure, you anatomized her assemblage, you
Dissevered her essentia. You sliver. stomp. stomp.   stomp.   stomp.
Butchers, you whetting your tools parading your
Flags (on)Woman Body, the ceremonial
Battlefield is. girl.body.child.body.body *anyone*
                          girlchildwoman *threat*
anyonecanunderstand.

In Nanking, an exhibition (20,000) of
Atrocity(child). Explicit(elders)Mutilation(*anyone*
Can)Systematic(woman)Violation (*anyone can*)(*understand*)

        Raped.to.Death.to
        raped.to.deathraped to

        Death.
        Woman, (who) comfort you?

In Nanking (   ).

Harringay Train Station
Found Poem

Ginger Whinger!
Ginger Minger!
Ginger Ninsa!
Ginger Crwger!
Gintas Virgis.

...

Synaesthesia

Collage prose poem composed from television advertisements, sitcoms and outdoor advertisements on billboards and other signage in North-Eastern U.S.A at the onset of the second Gulf War.

and there's this girl with muscular, chiselled, bulging arms, dead rats in the shape of a pentagram found in a basement. "I like to chop my macaroni up really small, so I need a really long lunch hour," *and the cleavage of art critics,* you sniff everything when you pick it up, even your bundle of keys. Hot wild girls are waiting for you to call, the grinder I pepper my food with.

my T.V. is a record player.

I ate so much, I don't know why, it was like I was stoned.

half-hour educational video on hot–tub ownership.

sometimes I eat my words. American Man Boy Love Association.

are you packing baby? *A famous poem is allowed to jump the queue,* our marriage is a burning house. David Hasselhoff.

have some cheese, what's the worst that could happen? I could die sir.

your wife is pretty thanks, I like your tie. Theres always one guy on the dancefloor, waggling solo. Barbituates. Ice sculpture. Together we're the land of milk and honey.

1-800 FREE LOVE. Lighter more convenient package; go-gurt. More anything? More everything. *How many girls auditioned to say These Are Very Dry on a fried chicken ad?* Dragging chairs. *What am I to do with this night?* Memorial service for a bird. I have over six hundred hours of television.

you did everything right, so what went wrong? Rich old frontin' fools. Don't say departed, 'cos that sounds like she might come back.

and this girl, someone was talking to her about fruit, mangoes and she said, "You mean like on Saturday Night Live?"

Lush. Assume position.

A water theme–park ad – This is why summer was invented! Oct 13, 2002 10:07 a.m.: BOMB BLAST IN BALI – in two nightclubs. Damn tootin', damn skippy.

In my country we dance on the graves of our enemies, in fact we dance on the graves of our friends, we just like to dance. *It is Halloween, and people are watching sitcoms about fictitious people celebrating Halloween.*

New! KY warming liquid, creates a warming sensation on contact. Hey I've tried everything else. *I have an illogical and unfair dislike for kids with skateboards.* So that's what a brain looks like on embalming fluid. Moisture Control Service. We Can Dry.

He calls a lifetime spent in front of the telly, marriage. Sock puppet psychosis. "I will be an enormous bulbous sex-god, and you won't be able to keep your hands off my lower lumbar." SCARY WATER? CALL US NOW!

He got shot up at a party. Not my pet, my animal companion. Do you want your anus stuffed with cotton? There's a new Lutheran in town and he's messing with the wrong farm boy. Overture.

Sprinkle my ashes in only the finest ashtrays all over New York. A little summin' summin'. Tricks.

END THE QUEST

YOU FOUND THE BEST.

I used to be with it, but then they changed what it is, so whatever I'm with isn't it, and 'it' is too wierd and scary to be with. *Generations continue to be raised on Led Zeppelin.* Why G.O.D? The universal language of shut-up. A five-minute pregnancy test, that's four minutes longer than it took you. *Television like a hearth.* I live a clean, blameless life.

Youth Oriented Product Positioning. *The future seems like a fortune concealed in a hollow cookie.* 10-10-987 a no-brainer. An eavesdropper never hears anything good about themselves. American Idol. *Deliverance.* "Slow incremental build-up". *'Cos that's what we need more 'no-brainers'.*

Brand new bomb EGBU-27 laser guided 1 metre accurate from up to 20,000 feet. Which one of you bitches is my mother? It may be the charm of fiction to devise a soft plan for us. Gifts from old boyfriends. I think your film can do with a little spicing up. Don't call me Barbie. Package target. Gas–and–go. War forecast for the Oscars: gold glitz/smoky eyes.

American Egg Board.

***

#poetry

Been waiting. 4 the rite tyme 2 "debut," my #poetry daughter 2 the #poetry 'scene-thing' where I cut my #poetry teeth tings ... like with my brutha A J when we , you know LOBSTER* ... Finally ... patiently waiting, years since she born ... likkle baby ... itty bitty, she wz three months n I remember, I remember went to Parliament, yah real Parliament for a #poetry ting ... met T. Atkins first #poetry person I saw post-birth ... never 4get he said 2 me "*Welcome To The Human Race,*" n so right he wz. So. Riiite. Mite dedicate a poem 2 him ... a book ... 'cos I do. I do feel mo' human now, innit? She likkle gal, My. Cherry Blossom. My. She make me human

So today. Now. Felt it was the right tyme. & for me, so great to go hear stuff. New stuff. Good. Stuff. Went 2 c, he-KAYO ... he ... a gud guy ... he. Gud stuff ... Lots of Loss. He young been thru a lot. I hear it in his #poetry. I heard it in my hrt. Loved the "Lumsdenesque of Lumsdenesque evenings" poem dedicated to. We know who. Gud guy. Another gud guy. & full circles we come around. get poetry, gift poetry. amiriite E-JB. Cherry B, she listen to Kayo. she. Even, she clap. Then she fall asleep in my arms for a bit n I felt that wz probz a gud nap. Listenin to the sonorous tones of. Yah. So. I feel it & I wonder am I feeling it for me, or for her. future, she. I. when.wz.am.

The poet is here referring to the cult reading series she curated with poet Anthony Joseph in the early 2000's called *La Langoustine Est Morte.* By mentioning it the poet is also acknowledging the great debt she owes to this event.

Thangka Number 1 "Bardo"
After The Garden of Earthly Delights – Heironymus Bosch
Written with John Alexander Arnold in Exquisite Corpse process

Is the sphere half empty?

O prison of profoundly inconceivable tortures, *to tackle the problem of death, one has to know all things as mere appearances to the mind, like illusions.* Let us adore you then wrap you all in the same black cabinet so your gaze not darken our dreams *one should become familiar with what to expect when they die,* The cranial merry-go-round of lusts, ambitions, judgements, that burn its victim from the inside out even while devouring it *whole so that one can deal with these illusions instead of being overwhelmed & confused by them.*

What horrible beauty will foment then be crushed & smothered by a global cycle of death by deluge?

Mind

Mind

Mind

Mind is constructing

Mind throws shapes

& shade

What bounty will flourish O paradise of unfathomable biodiversity, derived & distilled within a delicate cathedral of vats & beakers?

It is all, in Mind

Glistening cataclysm in a cosmic bauble from flood to flood O unquenchable thirsts quenched constantly By an endless font of strangest fruits!

There is no Heaven or Hell

It's all in your mind.

okgettin'offf 'bookgetttin'offffunkbookgettin'offnomatterhowmuchilovey'alligottagetOfff
fffffthisfunkinfuckbook4NOW,ONE DAY 4EVA..yehUheRdme

3:15
After Bernadette Mayer

an engaging periphery a remote location an unwise choice a clocked suburbia a waxwork antelope a crying ruby a sheet of cinnamon a stolen crane an answer a caucus a ranchero a night–light green saving you millions in pennies a surrogate landscape a graven lilly illuminati prosperity jinx high

at noon recycling cyclical by nature a gross lie caresses your face caked with mud from the Mojave incipient ending jack puffy fish lantern dinner removed twice like a cousin you've never met excuse me I must find the remote pedestal cavity nap-time for sugar women

I didn't wake up, I just happen to be awake.

Rainiarainiarain day to wear
Ill-fitting clothes, mismatched
      "todays the day. The convection
      heater that broke HAS to be
      thrown out".

Sakura is having imaginary
      Conversations with her real
      friends on her old baby
      monitor. Even though I offered
      her a real one with her
      birth friend, Zakir.

I've been walking around in
my panties & breasts out
for half an hour trying to
      get dressed to go to the
      doctor & the phone…
            's ringin
            & ringin-g
            & ringin-g-g

      like, so many times.

      Sakura says my nipples
      are like   tongues, stickingout.

No, seriously it's like this
  all things exist. The real
  shitty & the really good-
all at once –
    & you, just wait
    in mid
    – PAUSE –

  try not to run either way
      & get lost –

    That's it
     's like that
     jess like dat.

Retractable Patio Awning Systems
American Road Trip Collage Poem

sometimes a bar-tender and a librarian can serve the same purpose. PETS ON THE GRASS WILL BE SHOT. The fewer buildings you blow up the fewer you have to re-build. The possibilities are legion.

A mission to find the filthiest toilets in Hong Kong ... deliver a blow to your nose that will send bone-shards to your brain. *Mother Theresa, Lady Diana and Nusrat Fateh Ali all die in the same month.* I think I've dislocated my trouser furniture, the hands in a forensic photo holding the evidence.

MOAB missile. *Videogames as a case-study for the mutation of the violence gene in humans.* Coney Island White fish. You spend nine months in someone's stomach, of course you look awful when you come out.

Cultures are unique facets of the human imagination, they are not failed attempts at modernity. DA FOG HAS CLEARED. *Reclamation of memories, dreams, fantasy.* When you meet someone, you aren't meeting them you're meeting their representatives. *Writing on the backs of poems.*

The Natives are restless tonight. *There are no natives.*

IF YOU DRIVE
DRINK CULLIGANS.

Line

```
submit                  alley
      heat        shock
flash                   crack
        sickofdreams
submit                  journey
              a   x   i   s
malaise                 antiquity
        doubt      play
                        of swan
                        on swan
                        on swan
                        on swan
```

AUTOBIOGRAPHIA
an account of traumatic time spent in an archaic Catholic boarding school

Murree, blind
knife watch
drop dormitory brief
curtains awake

black, mary flat
black mary shuffle
feast board fancy
anne video gables

green pajamas, pajamas one
thousand steps chilblain
accuse foxy me also roxy
boxy,moxy, loxy

weevils, rice.

        *

sister, habit
goa from blood
suck girls we
devil michael

kills, red now
cubicle cubicle
jug wash stand
counterpane fold

one hundred years
for spirits *ghungru*
bathroom late alone
hear voice

ghungru, who is
pray curly clean
hair not puritan
exit character

building, plasticheart

*

bang, blackboard
mathematics hair
pins hide man
dress under

home, economics
win star win hepatitis
C home go lover
leave clutch kiss

hallway, secret

school boarding
orphan history soldiers
convent british

jesus,mary.

*

Mercedes, name
letter nun read
private my bitch

bitch, holy

fun, make personal
frog eyes my
mercedes trill
cut girls little

girls, fun

Berchmans,name
with irish wrinkle
puss alive me dug

head, grave.

*

Zarafshan, girl golden
family old twinkle
pants suck wrinkle
face puss eye

blue, gossip
p's q's watch
side my thorn

years threefromeleven
age, russiangirlchild
four. tiny
brutal Berchmans
heart chew

not, Zarafshan.

Poems for Eliot

Hair Blanket
Cold in The Dark

If it wasn't for you in silence, how

                          would I hear my heart beating, so
I know I'm still, living.

There's a (smell)

The earthy smell
programmed with life
in rude, vivid, alarmed

– No memory –

Dissection
Evaporation
retch
relay through body

if he only could describe the things that weighed
him down
Had I achieved a datastream of sighing
crescents, would you have allowed it?
The capacity for

all excelsior wounds   there is only one force sickness
point to this one
who is my true voice
I'm dark like a light

May 14
Moon waxing

This is for
all the
loss,
abandonment
& unrequited
love through
all ages,
all time,
forevermore.
This pain is

not for the
weak.

Loss

Longing
Remembrance

beef like a dog
rent, become junction
monster wrote epic
growing upper seize

"if the fabric of your hair
were consumed by fire
it would not burn"

"johnny depp talked of falling
In love with vanessa paradis'   back"

"I can't describe it"

"this spoke has no wheels"

"I let you kill me. Ad nauseum"

I let you kill me, Ad nauseum"

"I let you kill me. Ad nauseum"

"I want you to see them
                        The dances of the Storm Troopers"

I want to make you cry
like Morrissey wants to make you cry
on your unhappy birthday

's something like being trapped in an
infinite loop, loving you,

I feel like a monster has grown & she is beautiful

The way you love the sun
or the way carnivores talk of
"spare ribs," "rare bloody steak"
Or the way ants love
being ants or rain
loves falling or white

blood cells love infection or brown loves
being brown or stripes love being straight
or books love trees or
                flesh loves decay
                    and decay
                  loves stench
          and boiling water loves
                      heat and
          life loves death what
                does death love.
                        You, that's how I

Here are the combined memories
of two people. Here are the combined
memories. Here are the combined. Here
are the memories. Here is the memory.
Here is my memory of you, your memories
of me are different. I have no memory of
your memories. Whose life did I lead? Whose
memories do I remember. Who was in my
memories. Who are you? Who do I " remember"? What do I
"remember"? Did it even "happen"? Did two different
things happen? Your 'memory' of what happened and
my memory of what happened, and why aren't we together, now
                  and why aren't we
                  together now,

                  and why aren't we

                      together now
                      and why aren't

                        together now

                        together now
                          togethernow

She sleeps on her father's side of the bed
She hangs her left leg over the side of the bed
Like her father does.

I know for example right now if he is sleeping
in his studio apartment that nobody
can see, that if he's in bed, he's wearing
soft cotton jersey shorts, a t-shirt – a very old
rounded extreme blue t-shirt, it's
really old with a superman logo & he's
face downturned slightly & his left leg
will be cocked up, possibly hanging over
the edge of the bed.

       That's how she's sleeping right now. Like
       I mean this moment. What is that?
       What is that? Why do I know that?

       And only I know this. Only I see
       this. Why does it make me feel cracked
       in two parts, yet still walking.

           I don't know what's happening
           with my organs and stuff.

I am your mirror image.

You know this:
           I sleep on the right side of
           the bed with my right leg also
           cocked up and in a few hours
           she will, you will, and I will
           all be sleeping with our legs cocked
           up. It is a sequence. A pattern.

Your body melded with my body and we made a blueprint
For an earlobe. Her earlobe. The smallest, little
Structure hanging attached to a structure also
Small.

YOUR EARS
        MY EARS = HER e/A/R/S

knees, we made knees – a structure, we
made a blueprint for a structure contained in
a smallest of all structures – it's called D.N.A & it's
like under a microscope only visible and it's some
kind of fucking helix – we, you & me created
this helix – that's what she is – a wonder
helix containing all the information of the
universe – the stillness, the motion, the speed,
the temporal explanations of all things,
like you and me, our mystery. Our mystery
is drastically embedded, on an invisible
structure – unseen by Naked Eyes –
                        She is Unseen &
                                Yet I see her.
                                I see your D.N.A
                                I see my D.N.A
                                She is a wonder helix
                                She is a wonder helix

≫——→ ←——≪
I melt in   you melt in I
  I melt inyou melt in I
  I melt in youmelt in I
  I melt inyoumelt in I
  I meltinyoumeltin I
  ImeltinyoumeltinI   **IMIYMII**
                                       IMIYMII
                                       ≫——→ **MM** ←——≪

      eltnovelin
    m l y m t l

| It's a | smell |
There's	a smell
I	smell him
When I	smell him
a	smell

it's the smell of you, that endures
& it's only you, it's your smell
It's uncanny.
these things aren't grown
They appear.

It's personal

It's burning.

I live in this body
she lives in this body
they live in this body

we all live in this body

a word for: a feeling
that it's somebody's
birthday

A Year in Clouds
Poem Series

Friday June 27

No colour.
No identity.

Except what the light allows.

Dull, soggy striations resembling
Nothing or

Perhaps imagination
Illuminates if Mind
allows;
  mind says nothing.

Saturday June 28

Partitions of dark &
Lit – an enquiry

Today they grew from
No semblance, no
Differential at dawn

To visible ardour at dusk.

Sunday June 29

Compelled, I seek the clouds
at twilight, fixing
My sights.
Forgetting, that their visible
Absence ensures a better view

of the sky.

Monday June 30

I did not see
Any clouds
       today.

Therefore,
     there were no
         clouds.

Tuesday July 01

A shift barely audible in perception
     a form so faint
     camouflaged as light
          musical accompaniment, humming
             to a clear, brave stream.

Wednesday July 02

I have decided to watch the
Clouds, in real-time not
To be confused with
Recorded, Time for
Which we do not have
To wait, we push
Forward, bleat
Backwards;I missed
That moment, could
You play it Ag
ain, A   g
Ain   n
Or wait. Hold that
Moment please I
Want to examine it   closer

I say we Can
Prolong the mom
Ent ; remove   line
Ear planes   holding
it in:

                                                                time

Pause.
        Pause.
                Paws.
                        Pause
If   I   don't
Watch the clouds in
Real-time which is
Time, anyway without
Movement through

        Space – just I a
        Fixed   point am a
        Point fixed – if
        I don't   watch the
        Clouds in   real

                                                                time

        I will not see
        Them , transform &
        transform
                        &
                transform

        There is   no   such
        Thing   as   a cloud , just
        a   TRANSFORMATION <-> AXIS <-> WITHIN <->
        VARIABLE <-> ELEMENTS <->

                "if you shoot them
                        they shall not
                                bleed
                                burn or
                                break"

Thursday July 03

One moment its a heart

       The next, no longer one

             but a floating mess.

Friday July 04

What goes on
Behind the thickening panopoly of cloud

What is it
Being hidden from sight?

Is it a co-operation
Between sky-space & cloud-time?

What is it the clouds
Are masquerading as?

Or is the dance of Salome
To steady us,

Too frail to absorb
the full limit of colour
in the sky.

We stand facing each
Other, wordless &

I am uncertain who
is moving slower.

Saturday July 05

I am writing about
clouds of the day before the
day before.
Memory-clouds.

Clouds in retrospect

I took photographs imagining
I would write about them

But a cloud in retrospect
Is not cloud at all

        just an after-image.

Sunday July 06

Today, I am in a state of rebellion against
myself, clouds especially

myself.

Monday July 07

a shoaling miasma

of variform   apparitions

       scrolling like
           ticker-tape
        saying nothing.

*

www.ingramcontent.com/pod-product-compliance
Lightning Source LLC
Chambersburg PA
CBHW052342100426
42736CB00047B/3434